Presentation by *BookLeaf Publishing*

Web: www.bookleafpub.com

E-mail: info@bookleafpub.com

ISBN: 9789358361445

First edition 2021

IDLING

Matt James Adam

BookLeaf Publishing

India | USA | UK

For Dana, when I am said and done, you'll still be the breath in my lung.

ACKNOWLEDGEMENT

Writing this book has been as challenging as it has been rewarding. Prolonged periods of isolation from friends, family and at times the outside world, has given me more to write about than I'd care to, but with very little motivation to do so.

Dana, for your ardent support and subtle barbs, that keep me on my toes, always moving forward. Your plethora of advice has been invaluable. Thank you, my love. Without you, my life has no art.

Even with all the time we've spent apart, you constantly find ways to flood my heart.

I'm forever indebted to Tracy, who has always encouraged my creativity and who sent me on this journey. Our talks, and walks, have been as cherished to me as your perspective and the positivity exude.

With some of these works being incredibly personal I found it difficult to share them with anyone, let alone close friends. Nicole thank you, for 'allowing' me to flick through pieces without warning and always being a friend I could trust with my worlds. Your feedback has meant a great deal to me throughout this process.

Lastly, I want to thank Dad, Alex, Isobella, Xavier and the people they love, who have become just as dear to me. You're all individually spectacular people. Mum, I find myself grateful for you every single day. When I'm cold, hungry, and alone, at my nadir, it's thought of us all together that keep me warm.

NORA

She says don't you worry boy

The sun will rise, the dark will fall

I shield my eyes from the creeping glare

But I can't hold

the horizons stare.

COLOUR-BLIND

The sound of her indignation

Pulls at the corner of my lips

Soundly reproved for calling her bed spread red

A coy smile breaks her faux frustration

There's nothing sexier than her quips

Or the sweat dripping from her hips

Three deliberate steps

Towards her sheer blue dress

Backlit in the dim moon grin

My hands around her shape

Thumbs coasting down her skin

In this fleeting ceaseless embrace

Rushing blood

Drowning out

Her playlist and my doubts

Willingly imprisoned

In the creases

Of her vermillion linen.

EARTH

3

I could live three times longer than I spent with my mother

I've lost my lifeline.

What defines a lifetime

Will I remember her face when they put me in a home

How she commanded a room even complete alone

Took every risk to change my life for the better

Even if I'd hate her.

Whatever the weather

She'd glow in my life so I could always feel my toes,

Buried in the earth.

That's now interred

all I know.

DRINKING BUDDIES

4

Soft glows splash the tired lacquered top,

Of this charcoal oak elbow prop.

Bereft of spills presently,

But with a persistent memory.

So these spirits linger

Company for my entropy.

Whiskey. Irish. Two fingers.

To fix their mouths shut chemically.

Alas, the medicine is reticent,

To fight off all I've jettisoned.

Fuck it, sit. Let's reminisce.

Tell me everything I missed,

Since yesterday.

ETCHES AND OUTFLOWS

How far we've come

From carving pseudonyms

In these rot soaked limbs

Fed by a bleeding drum

A crystal fountain of truth

Washes the ink from our leather

The names we thought were forever

Dilute with the vermouth

Little did we know those stains

Our polished skin will lament

Danced along the cement

Drained, into a mundane sea

of missed opportunities.

UNARMED

8

I only dream when I'm awake.

In chaos or tranquillity

It does little more than sedate

My diminishing abilities.

A verdant canopy shielding impotence

My ego projects confidence

Adroit in its defence

At least, of the demons I'm cognizant.

So I sit in the shade

Of my unopened curtains

Remembering the blades

I once wielded, instead of this bourbon.

One meal a day, couch-bound

Chestnut liquor imbued

Swallowed in the sound

Of silence melting into solitude.

SPLINTER

Is time anymore

than the tides washing the shore.

Can it heal the failing wings

That carry these wanton limbs

A stagnant sky

A starless sea

Rudderless in the debris

Of two ships that didn't miss

Lips turning blue in this abyss

Still stained with your kiss

A splinter underneath my skin

From now until Le Fin.

TRANSPARENCY

Comfortable deception

Stag at another wedding reception,

Polite deference, somewhat disingenuous

To the stranger across the table

Who thirsts for more of me than is available

Losing my fluid shape, challenged without escape

Transfixed by the potency of her adamant gaze

She cuts thru the hollow rows of my faux esoteric maze

I'll never be the ocean

An undulating desert of mystique

While she can see right to the bottom

Pull the plug with any word she speaks

It's a wonder I'm still alive

Without your touch that set me alight

Even in the middle of the day

She can tell, meteors from satellites

12

LOVE AND WAR

Too preoccupied burying your point into my chest

To hear mine.

Ensanguined fingers in your ears

Tongue cocked, to fire detritus

Of previous fights

Across a deepening divide.

Ripping out the stitches

Til the trickle becomes a flood

My bucket can't keep up

Bailing out the blood

Drowning in our shared misery

Choking on everything I should've said

Until you take pity

And grab the needle and thread.

REFILL

14

With an empty glass and a liquid heart

I dream of proving to the world that I exist

But I can't tell talent and pot-valour apart

As I sip at the melting ice, vanquished.

SKYLINE

I like to look up

At the dilapidated facades

Of once ordinary buildings

Sometimes, for a reprieve

From all life's little delights

To remind myself that not matter our condition

We can survive a lack of supervision

Other times,

for a sturdy beam.

BAKE

16

Love,

does not a relationship make.

It is an ingredient

but not the whole cake.

INSOMNIA

Lost in midnights silhouette

My anxieties project bold headlines

For the late night gazette

…Puns could be snappier

The subtle depths of quiet

Fold into the dark calm

A momentary relief

Before waking in alarm.

BRIDIE

Hand painted shades

Complete the cascade of missing frames

Between the vodka lemonade

And dawns warmth on my bedroom panes

Flickering projections

From passing train cars

Doomed connections

Heading in the wrong direction

In contrast,

Try as I may, to say au revoir

I'm rapt in the shadow cast

By blonde haired girl playing guitar.

I DIDN'T GET HER NAME

19

The more she drinks the less she hides it

A fleeting glance has sunk into a lascivious leer

I smile to be polite, and she looks fun so fuck it

She's dancing like I'm watching,

I'm not.

PERSPECTIVE

Are our enemies

Anymore

Than reflections

Of our own entities

TUESDAYS

21

There's no end to this ocean spray

Dry's my skin and draws from my soul

The will to overcome constant waves

Of listless chaos, without land or atoll.

As I'm beaten and strewn about the deck

Of this leaking wreck

I long for the stars, distant and quiet

Far from the fury

Of this silent riot.

DRIFTWOOD

Driftwood, slick with insobriety

Lashed by mighty waves

Warped by the heave of society

Now, the currents misbehave.

Wrenched from the mire

Handpicked for its splintered facade

Dressed to suppress all that's been chewed

Instead of buried in the warmth of a campfire

To burn all I've imbued

Tossed back to the sea

When the edges won't smooth

And the plane can't content with the stains

Of my youth.

23

DIVORCE

24

Festering limbs, severed on a whim

In spite of their efforts to bring us together

In this game of how much can you take

We rely on sleep to convalesce all we choose to repress

Yet, we only dream post daybreak.

DANA

25

We spent two weeks

In summer heat

Island hopping Cocktail's flowing

I knew I could spend the rest of my life with you.

You flew home,

To pack your things

A pandemic hit

Clipped our wings

It's been sixteen months

Without your touch

But I can't give up

Not on you.

Not on us.

I'll break every rule I'll wait and wait and wait and wait

I have been

Ever since we met

Those years ago

On sunset.

DEPTHS

Braced my body for decay

Hardened my gaze, while others prayed

Prepared to steal hope, kept lock away,

in the chest of the sea.

One final breath, then I leapt.

A crowd rushed to the edge

Surveyed with great angst, for an entire age

Trying to spy a telling spray

Against the backdrop of the thrashing waves

Wrists were wrung

Watches checked, calculations done

Coins were spun, end over end

On the chance I had won

The water did not relent

Their shoes began to soak

Red running rings, around their eyes

From their daydreams they slowly awoke

Not a sound left their lips

As they did all silently attest

That I never surfaced

From her black depths.

THE EVERGLADE

29

Flecks of charcoal line the resplendent grass.

Through the field of stone, a barefoot forged path

While Silence reigned in the sun drenched malaise

I retrace the climbing steps the morphine took

Hands outstretched to catch the debris of our yesterday's

As they float down and flood the ground, like a winter tree shook

But it's the aroma of the failed hospital disinfectant that lingers

Disregarding the tantrums and prays of my dry whispers

My cancer-less husk a hedonistic paradise for disease

Unlike the demons I survived, these are not in my mind

This glade will fill, until neither are you.

ANNIE

A smile held together

with duct tape and gin

A burst of light

shades all manner of sin

The definition of her cheeks

Belie the tension in her breath

avoiding eye contact,

as his hand finds the small of her back.

Guises of forged glee

Haunting the entry hall

Mirrored perspectives of two women, stalled

Both unable to flee

SKIN AND BLISTER

Skin and blisters

From these weary hands

Languid and bruised

Calloused but true

This compass I give to you

It will not point north, south, east or west.

But follows instead the beat

That echoes from within

The quite machinery of your chest

When your journey takes you

Beneath the towering masses

Of the tallest alps

Turn to this compass for your guide

Close your eyes and let it help

Feel the air around you

32

This path is ancient

A fixture of life

Follow your needle true

The other side you'll come thru

In the darkest hues, of those starless seas

When it gets harder to breathe,

Grip tight to this compass

It's weathered disguise

A facade full of regard

Worn, beaten and scarred,

Its organs will not think twice, remain precise

Sail you through, into stellar lights

And If an hour nears

Any given year

That leaves you gripped in fear

Call my name

I'll be here.

REFLECTIONS OF SARAH

35

Her perilous quips

To join her in the abyss

Her grin equal to the sin

Leaves me entrance and lingering

Yet still I turn to go,

Until I catch her in the window

Silent, loud, desperate but proud.

Shouts of stop become quite clear

For a moment

Until the rushing wind is all I hear.

NEVER LUCKY

36

A lack of savoir-faire

As lucky as a Baudelaire

And the fitting the irony

Of spiralling while idling

At least today I can blame my life on the fact

Mercury is in Gatorade

37

More of an excuse to pat her ass

Than a conversation spark

"Misery. My tea leaves decree."

Her focus unfazed as she shuffles past

Searching for the coffee in a daze

With a trite sigh and slight frown

She reprises

"Love, you've got them upside-down"

FLOWERS

38

Blissfully unaware

The boy races around the frantic kitchen

hands suctioned to his face, with both covered and closed eyes

"you can't see me if I can't see you"

Narrowly avoiding all manor dangers

as he plays the entertainer

Now he can't understand

the flowers sleeping in her hand

from fields where they toiled

only to be buried in soil

"Dad, why grow them at all?"

"It takes great courage to grow, to be strong and loud.

They coloured this world brighter

and now make us smile whenever we look at the clouds"

Unperturbed, he makes one final trip

To the flowers in her grip.

"You can't see me if I can't see you"

"You can't see me if I can't see you"

SIDES OF THE INDIVISIBLE

Soundless voice

The limpid smoke

Clinging to the fabric

Of which I'm made

Raucous and apathetic

Indivisibly entwined

Could a bullet's kiss

Even separate us

BREACH

Wrestling for control with eyes closed,

my muted fists making no indent.

No signs of life, to fight this retrograde,

while others float, I am weighed.

Til an inexplicable hope - internally maligned - swims in my breast,
and impedes the descent.

From the pastel depths towards the rugged seascape, I reorient.

Propelled by the lightness of my chest the surface draws close,

as these stagnant fist, unfurl, become verbose.

Impetuous, they hack like scythes racing against the ephemeral
twilight.

Alas, they do little but force feed the embers in my lungs, burning
the last of the oxygen.

A desperate siege, undone.

Salvation out of reach

As my fingertips breach.